# TRADE & WARFARE

## ROBERT HULL

# FRANKLIN WATTS
## A Division of Grolier Publishing
NEW YORK • LONDON • HONG KONG • SYDNEY
DANBURY, CONNECTICUT

Acknowledgements: AKG London cover l (Louvre, Paris/
E. Lessing), tr (Staatl. Antikenslg, & Glyptothek., Munich), br
(Louvre, Paris/E. Lessing), pp. 2-3 (E. Lessing), 4t (National
Archeological Museum, Athens), 5t (Haaretz Museum, Tel
Aviv), 5b (Israel Museum (IDAM), Jerusalem/E. Lessing), 6b
(National Maritime Museum, Haifa/E. Lessing), 7t
(E. Lessing), 7b (National Archeological Museum, Beirut/
E. Lessing), 8 (Staatl. Antikenslg, & Glyptothek., Munich),
12t (Delphi Museum/E. Lessing), 13bl (E. Lessing), 14t
(Akademie den Bildenden Kuenste/E. Lessing), 15t (Louvre,
Paris/E. Lessing), 15cr (National Archeological Museum,
Athens/E. Lessing), 15b (British Museum/E. Lessing), 16t
(E. Lessing), 16b (Louvre, Paris/E. Lessing), 17t (Louvre,
Paris), 19t (British Museum/E. Lessing), 20b (Louvre, Paris/
E. Lessing), 21 (SMPK, Antidenmuseum, Berlin), 22 (Louvre,
Paris/E. Lessing), 24t (Louvre, Paris/E. Lessing), 24b
(E. Lessing), 25 (Musée Vivenel, Compiegne), 26r (Pergamon
Museum), 26l (E. Lessing), 27r (Museé Vivenel, Compiegne/
E. Lessing), 28t (Bibliotheque Nationale, Paris), 28b
(National Museum of Archeology, Naples), 29 (Archeological
Museum, Istanbul/E. Lessing);
Ancient Art and Architecture Collection pp. 11b (Brian
Wilson), 12b (Ronald Sheridan), 19b (Ronald Sheridan);
Automobile Association Photo Library pp. 15cl, 18r; e.t.
Archive pp. 6t (National Museum, Athens), 13tr (Louvre,
Paris), 14b (Acropolis Museum, Athens), 18l (Acheological
Museum, Ferrara), 20t (Archeological Museum, Salonica);
Robert Harding Picture Library p. 10; John Heseltine p. 11t;
Robert Hull p. 13tl; Hulton Getty Collection p. 27l;
Hutchison Picture Library p. 17b (Nick Haslam);
Travel Ink pp. 9l (Nigel Bowen-Morris), 9r (Rawdon Wyatt).

Series editor: Rachel Cooke
Designer: White Design
Consultant: Dr Anne Millard
Picture research: Susan Mennell
Artwork: Peter Bull Artists

First published in 1999 by Franklin Watts

First American edition 1999
by Franklin Watts
A Division of Grolier Publishing
90 Sherman Turnpike
Danbury, CT 06816

Visit Franklin Watts on the Internet at:
http://publishing.grolier.com

ISBN:    0-531-14540-9 (lib. bdg.)
         0-531-15384-3 (pbk.)

A CIP catalog record for this book
is available from the Library of Congress

# CONTENTS

# EARLY TRADE

**W**ith a long coastline and many islands, ancient Greece was always a land of travelers. They sailed long distances to exchange goods peacefully, or to raid and plunder. They traveled to find new homes, and they spread Greek ideas through the ancient world.

A 13th-century B.C. fresco from the island of Thera (Santorini) showing Minoan boats leaving port.

## Ancient Sea Traders

As early as about 8000 B.C., Greeks were criss-crossing the Aegean Sea to mine rock or flint on various islands. By about 3000 B.C., Greek metalworkers were making bronze, using copper from Cyprus and Sardinia and tin from the east and the west.

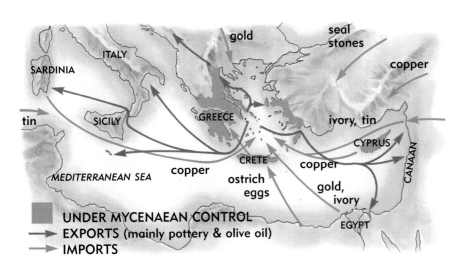

ITALY
SARDINIA
gold
seal stones
copper
tin
SICILY
GREECE
ivory, tin
CYPRUS
CRETE
copper
CANAAN
MEDITERRANEAN SEA
copper
ostrich eggs
gold, ivory
EGYPT

■ UNDER MYCENAEAN CONTROL
➤ EXPORTS (mainly pottery & olive oil)
➤ IMPORTS

Under the Minoans, Crete was the first great center of trade. Their ships carried olive oil and other goods south to Egypt and all around the eastern Mediterranean. There are written records, on clay tablets, of their trade and their local taxes.

This map shows early Minoan and Mycenaean trade links.

## The Mycenaeans

From about 1500 B.C., Mycenaeans from mainland Greece took over from the Minoans as the main traders in the area. Mycenaean kings exchanged gifts peacefully with Egyptian pharaohs. The Greeks took olive oil, wine, and pottery and in return received alabaster, gold, ivory, and ostrich eggs.

Other Mycenaean merchants went to Babylon, Thrace, and the Black Sea. Bits of their pottery have been found in Libya, Israel, Sardinia, and even Italy.

**archaeologist:** Our modern word means someone who studies the remains of the past. It comes from two Greek words: *archai* – the beginning – and *logos* – words.

A bronze necklace made in Mycenae between 1550 and 1200 B.C. It was found in modern Israel.

## THEIR OWN WORDS

In this letter a Cypriot king of about 1300 B.C. orders goods from the king of Egypt.

*"A message from the King of Cyprus to the King of Egypt. My brother, I send a messenger to you with 100 talents of copper. Will your messenger please bring me one ebony bed trimmed with gold, one chariot with two horses, fourteen beams of ebony, and some bales of the finest linen."*

## The Dark Age Begins

But around 1250 B.C., the early Greek cities were burned and destroyed. Famine may have caused Greeks from the islands or the colonies of what is now Turkey to attack the mainland. Over the next 150 years the cities disappeared, writing was forgotten, and the Greeks no longer traveled as they once had. The Dark Age had begun.

This Mycenaean goblet was exported from mainland Greece to Canaan (the Near East).

# AFTER the DARK AGE

**D**uring the Dark Age, there was hardly any new building in stone or brick, and not much artistic craft work. Greeks traveled and traded much less and had much less contact with the rest of the world.

## Reviving Greece

City life continued in Athens and at places such as Lefkandi on the island of Euboea. Pottery was still made in many towns. The Greeks kept up some trade, especially with Cyprus, where iron objects such as knives and axes were made. These hard new iron axes cut down trees more quickly than bronze axes, so ships could be built more easily.

Pottery, decorated with geometric designs as on this 9th-century B.C. vase, formed an important part of the re-emerging Greek trade.

From the 8th century B.C., the Greek city of Corinth exported vases like this one, in ships like those painted on its side.

Soon more Greeks began to travel again, searching for metals such as tin and copper, selling pottery, and exploring. Communities grew larger. From about 800 B.C., the Greeks combined cities and their surrounding farmland into "city-states." With busy city-states came more travel and trade.

## Competition

During the Dark Age, the Phoenicians — the Canaanite people who lived along the coast of modern Lebanon — had taken over from the Mycenaean Greeks as the main traders in the area.

But Greek traders began to rival them again. They settled at Al Mina in Syria, sending wine and oil by river and overland to Babylon, and taking home fine fabrics, ivory, gold, tin, and slaves — just as the Mycenaeans had done. They set up trading centers at Naucratis in Egypt and Cyrene in north Africa.

The remains of a Phoenician temple at Byblos, in modern Lebanon.

This Phoenician silver coin shows a ship and hippocamp (a type of sea-monster).

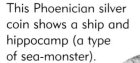

During the Dark Age, the Mycenaean way of writing and keeping records had been forgotten. But new ideas are carried by trade and travel. When some Phoenicians came to Greece, says Herodotus, "They brought the alphabet, which … had not been known to the Greeks… The Greeks who lived amongst the Phoenicians learned the alphabet from them, making a few changes in the form of the letters…" The Romans in turn adapted the Greek alphabet and this became our own.

## Plunder or Fair Exchange

Some trade was really plunder, stolen by acts of piracy or in minor skirmishes. Most trade was barter — peacefully swapping things, perhaps on the beach. Merchants from Babylon and beyond laid out their precious goods and took the Greeks' specialities in exchange.

# SHIPS AND SEA TRAVEL

o the Greeks, ships and sailing were vital.
Without ships, the Greeks could not move
from island to island for trade, travel, or warfare.
Themistokles, a famous leader, said, "So long as
we have our ships, we Athenians have a city."

**anchor:** Our word
"anchor" is almost the
same as the Greek
word *ankyra*, meaning
anchor or hook.

## Ships

From early times, ships were built
of oak, fir, or poplar, with a
supple mast of fir. They were
crescent-shaped, with a
tall stern. Warships were
narrow for speed and
had rowers as well as
a mast; merchant
ships were wider
and relied on sails
and a steering oar.
The ships were
anchored with
large stones.

In this 6th-century B.C. drinking
cup, the god Dionysus travels
in a Greek merchant ship. It is
attacked by pirates, who are
magically turned into dolphins,
while the mast becomes a vine.

8

## The Weather

Ships only sailed when the weather was good, between late spring and early autumn. Even then, sailing could be dangerous. Storms blew up, and there was no compass or sextant for navigation — only the sun and stars, and landmarks. So most Greek ships, which were small and slow anyway and couldn't sail against headwinds, stayed close to land, carrying goods locally from one harbor to the next.

The broken, rocky coastline of Greece was hard to navigate. At the top of this headland, Cape Souniun, is a temple to Poseidon, god of the sea. Greek sailors would pray to him for a safe journey.

## ▪▪▪ LEGACY ▪▪▪

Sea travel is as much a part of modern Greece as it was 2,000 years ago. At harbors such as Piraeus (pictured above) and Patras, you can see ships from every corner of the Mediterranean, just as in ancient times. From all over Europe, trucks, buses, and cars arrive in Patras on the big Greek ferries from Italy. Cars and trucks travel to the islands by boat, and so does most traffic between north and south Greece.

## Traveling Overland

Overland transport was expensive and difficult in a land of mountains and rough tracks. Mule teams and ox carts were slow, but merchants did go overland when they had to. Journeys west from Athens often avoided going around the southern tip of the Peloponnese; instead, merchants hauled boats overland along a stone track — a *diolchos* — across the thin land-bridge that joined the Peloponnese to the rest of Greece.

# GREEK COLONIES

**B**etween about 800 and 500 B.C., many Greeks sailed away to new homes. They went west to Italy and Sicily, south to Africa, and north to Thrace and Macedonia and the Black Sea.

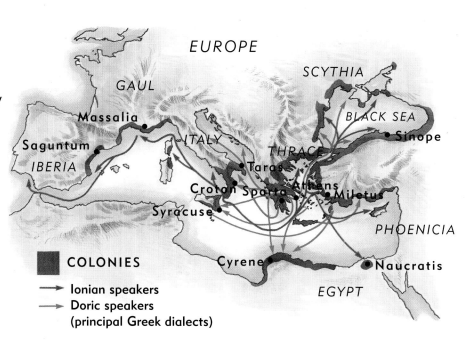

EUROPE

SCYTHIA

GAUL

Massalia

BLACK SEA

Saguntum

Sinope

IBERIA

ITALY

THRACE

Taras

Croton Sparta Athens Miletus

Syracuse

PHOENICIA

COLONIES

Cyrene

Naucratis

→ Ionian speakers
→ Doric speakers
(principal Greek dialects)

EGYPT

## Invading Colonists

The Greeks went for many reasons — quarrels in the city, overcrowding (due to a rapid population growth), famine, and greed. Many settlements were like invasions. In Sicily, Greek colonists drove out the local Sicel people to found Naxos, then built thick walls for protection.

Colonists were often looking for slaves or precious metals. In 600 B.C., the Phocians from central Greece founded Massalia (modern Marseilles), took control of the tin trade with Britain, and sent slaves to Greece from the local tribes.

Modern Marseilles, originally the Greek colony Massalia, and still one of the busiest ports in the Mediterranean.

## "Great Greece"

Many Greeks settled in Sicily and southern Italy – *Magna Graecia*, or "Great Greece." The area became very prosperous, as it had rich agricultural land and could sell much cheese and pork to Greece. Syracuse became the biggest city in the Greek world.

## THEIR OWN WORDS

One later Roman writer, Justinus, thought that the coming of the Greek colonists was a very good thing for the people of Gaul (in this case, France and Spain):

*"From the Greeks the Gauls learned a more civilized way of life... They began tilling their fields and walling their towns. They began to live according to the law, and grow vines and olives... It seemed they had become part of Greece, not that Greece had colonized Gaul."*

The Greeks built temples in their colonies. This is the Temple of Concord at Agrigento on Sicily.

Greek colonies often minted their own coins. This one from Tarentum in Italy shows its founder, Taras, arriving on a dolphin.

## Trade and Conflict

New settlements kept up close links with the mother cities; and when colonies sent out their own colonists, the founder had to be from the mother city, too. Trading was an important part of the link. When colonists from Miletus founded cities on the coasts of the Black Sea, Milesian goods were exported there, in return for local products.

Along with the trade was plenty of fighting. In Sicily the Greeks fought the Carthaginians. Greek fought Greek, too. In 520 B.C., the Italian Greek city of Croton destoyed a wealthy neighboring city, Sybaris.

# PIRATES AND PLUNDER

On their expeditions the early Greeks might barter wine and oil for things like copper and tin. But they might also raid, kidnap, and plunder to get what they wanted. Trade, war, plunder, and piracy were often closely linked; one could easily turn into the other.

**pirate:** We get our word "pirate" from the Greek word *peirates*, meaning a "sea-robber."

## Piracy or War?

It was sometimes hard to tell the difference between war and piracy. Homer's noble hero, Odysseus, sometimes behaved like a pirate. He attacked a people called the Kikones, killed the men and made slaves of the women. He also pretended to have been a well-known Cretan pirate.

Piracy was a weapon of war, too. In one war the Athenians carried out acts of piracy and plunder against their enemy, who had previously kidnapped Athenian merchants. Athenian ships seized fishing boats and ships carrying corn.

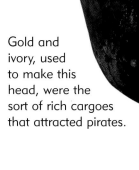

Gold and ivory, used to make this head, were the sort of rich cargoes that attracted pirates.

A pirate attack? A heavy grain ship is about to be rammed by a light-weight warship.

## The Pirate Problem

Pirates were always a problem for Greek traders, especially in the west, but also in the north, near Thrace and in the Black Sea. There were treaties — legal arrangements — between cities to try to stamp it out. In the 4th century B.C., Philip II of Macedon, who became the conqueror of all Greece, quarrelled with the Athenians because they were not doing enough to clear the seas of pirates.

But piracy couldn't be stopped. The pirates had too many bases in the Greek world, and pirate plunder made some cities prosperous, especially those that relied on the slave trade. The island of Aegina, for instance, had few riches of its own but grew very prosperous through piracy.

The narrow streets that lead to many Greek harbors were originally a defense against pirates.

A bronze statuette of an African slave, perhaps captured in a Greek raid (right).

Money from piracy helped build the temple of Athena on Aegina (left).

### THEIR OWN WORDS

When Alexander the Great captured a pirate and threatened to put him to death, the pirate defended himself by saying: *"Because I raid with a small boat I'm called a pirate. You do the same thing with a large army and you're called an emperor."*

# TRADE INSIDE GREECE

**A**s the cities of Greece grew bigger and richer, they began to trade more. Even wars didn't stop trade; Greek wars were not continuous, and brief battles interfered no longer than bouts of bad weather.

A 6th-century B.C. vase painting of traders carrying and weighing cloth.

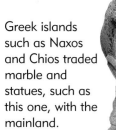

Greek islands such as Naxos and Chios traded marble and statues, such as this one, with the mainland.

## Business as Usual

Once a land of separate small communities, by 600 B.C. Greece again became a busy trading area. City traded with city, island with island. They traded in building materials, furniture, cloth, food, and drink. Fine new harbors were built, on Samos for instance, and at Piraeus, the port for Athens. Many islands and cities had their specialities. For example, the island of Cos was famous for its fine fabrics.

**drachma:** In modern Greece, money is still counted in drachmas, a word that comes from the ancient Greek *drakh*, meaning "grasp." Drachma meant a handful — probably of 6 bits of iron.

## Athens, the Business Center

Athens was the busiest city for Greek trade. It had special markets for wine, olive oil, and cheese; for tanners of leather; honey sellers; makers of bedding and couches. And there were areas for potters' and bronze-casters' shops. There was even a "Thieves' Harbor" near Piraeus, where shady or illegal trade took place.

7th-century B.C. tablet showing a potter working at his wheel.

**Visitors to Greece today can buy many things that were sold in the 5th century B.C.: olives and olive oil from Attica or Kalamata, wine from Thasos or Cephalonia, cheeses, Greek honey, beautiful fabrics and laces, small pots of perfumed oil, and so on. In Athens many of these items can be bought on Odos Pandrosou (shown above) and Odos Hephaestou — two streets in a warren of lanes and passages that have been part of the same market areas for 2000 years.**

## Bankers

Bankers did their business in Athens, too. Money was only invented in the 6th century B.C. (in Lydia). Using money, rather than doing exchanges, made trade and banking easier. That said, each city in Greece had their own style of coins, so money changers and bankers needed to sort it all out.

A stamp for minting an Athenian coin. It shows the owl, sacred to Athena

One important kind of banking was lending to merchants, to hire ships and buy cargoes. Merchants paid high rates of interest, especially if the ship was to sail where pirates were busy. Unscrupulous merchants sometimes took their money and vanished. Many ships sank "accidentally."

A 4th-century B.C. 4-drachma coin from the colony of Ephesos on the coast of modern Turkey. The bee was the symbol of Ephesos.

# IMPORTS AND EXPORTS

Lions of Naxos marble guard the Sacred Way on Delos, the island sacred to Apollo. The lions show an Egyptian influence, probably resulting from trading contacts.

**M**erchants carried goods from the rich Greek cities to countries outside the Greek world. They sailed to Egypt, Macedonia, and Thrace, to Italy and the lands around the Black Sea.

In the 7th century B.C., Corinth exported specialty perfume containers, like this owl-shaped one.

## Selling and Buying

These countries wanted many things from Greece: olive oil, wine, silver, pottery, sculpture, furniture, clothing, and books. On the return journeys merchant ships brought things the Greeks didn't produce enough of themselves: timber (from Macedonia), corn (from the Black Sea), and various luxury items. Slaves could be sold at a good price in the Greek homeland. From the east came perfume and spices; from Egypt, wheat, linen, papyrus, and precious things.

## Wheat

Many Greek cities did not grow enough wheat. Athens always needed grain. It came at first from Egypt and Sicily, then from the Black Sea. For long periods, the Athenians controlled the grain route from the Black Sea. They built military fortresses on its northern coast, and collected a 10 percent toll on ships passing through the narrow Hellespont channel that joined the Black Sea with the Aegean. In wartime, escort ships guarded the grain ships.

Wine was another Greek export. This 6th-century B.C. vase shows the grape harvest.

**bible:** One product that the Greeks sent abroad was books. The word "bible," which we use to describe a big authoritative book or the sacred writings of Christianity, The Bible, comes from the Greek word for book, *biblion*.

## A Weapon of War

Sparta, often Athens' enemy, usually had plenty of wheat. It came from Messenia, the country farmed by Sparta's semi-slave — *helot* — population. It was a great advantage in wartime; cities won wars by cutting off the enemy's food supply. Timber, which by the 6th century B.C. was also scarce in Greece, was an important import and, like wheat, the trade became a weapon in war.

Greek olive groves produced vast amounts of olives and olive oil for export. They still do today.

# QUARRELSOME GREEKS

**G**reek wars were not like modern wars, widely spread and continuous. Even long wars were mainly on-and-off struggles, and most were soon over. But war was an important part of Greek life, and most Greek men could expect to be involved in a war at some time or other.

A soldier leaving for war has shaken hands with his father and faces his mother.

In times of war, the people of Corinth retreated to their high fortified acropolis.

**kudos:** This word has come straight from Greek into English. In Greek it meant fame or glory, usually achieved in battle, while in English, we use it to mean the credit you earn when you've done something well — "brownie points."

## The Causes of War

Greeks went to war for different reasons. They invaded parts of Africa, Asia, and Europe — for land, slaves, precious metals, and trade. They fought to defend Greece against invaders. And they regularly fought each other, city against city, often to keep control of a trade — in timber, wheat, or metals. Then when Athens was very powerful, there were wars between her and the cities that revolted against her control.

## Agricultural Land

Many quarrels between neighboring city-states were about farmland, and because farmer-soldiers didn't want to guard distant borders, or spend much time fighting, disputes were settled by arranged battles, usually on flat land not used for farming. They often tried to have a fighting season after the harvest.

A 6th-century B.C. vase picture of two warriors fighting.

## Sparta

For most citizen soldiers, war interrupted work. In Sparta it was different. Spartan citizens were not allowed to work. They were permanently ready for battle. From the age of seven, boys lived away from home, "boarding" in military style schools, and men spent more time in barracks than at home.

The Spartans' farming was done for them by Messenian *helots*, who had lost their freedom to Sparta in a war.

A 6th-century B.C. bronze figure of a Spartan soldier.

### THEIR OWN WORDS

It was a disgrace for a Spartan soldier to lose his shield (that is, run away from battle):

*"Come home with your shield — or on it,"* one tough Spartan mother is supposed to have said to her departing soldier son.

A Spartan poet says,
*"He who falls in the front of the line and loses his life brings honor to his city, his family, and his father."*

# WAR ON LAND

In most states, it was Greek citizens in the assembly who decided on a war, and citizens who fought in it, together on foot, with their own armor and supplies.

## Hoplites

The armor of these citizen-soldiers — hoplites — was bulky and heavy. It consisted of a long spear, a short sword, a wooden shield with a bronze rim, a bronze helmet, a bronze body-protector, and leg-guards. It all came to about half the weight of a man, so one of the hoplite's slaves usually carried it — with their rations — to the battleground. The armor was expensive and each soldier bought his own, so hoplite soldiers were mainly well-off citizens, often farmers.

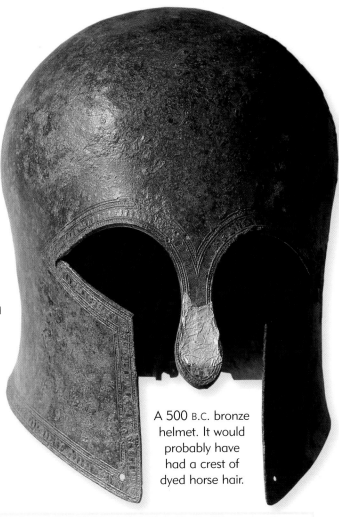

A 500 B.C. bronze helmet. It would probably have had a crest of dyed horse hair.

A running hoplite carrying his helmet and armor.

## THEIR OWN WORDS

Herodotus describes an unusual hoplite tactic that the Spartans used against the Persians:

*"The Spartans had a brilliant idea… They all turned their backs and ran, pretending to be running for their lives. The Persians charged, screaming and banging their shields, but just as the gap closed the Spartans turned to face them and dealt them terrible havoc."*

## Fighting in Formation

Infantry in Greek armies fought in a phalanx — a densely-packed square that attacked at a running trot. The thud when one phalanx smashed into another must have been audible on mountain tops. Then came the terrible push. If the first rank fell, the second took over, walking over the dead. But because Greek wars were not continuous and hoplite battles were restricted, casualties were not as high as in modern wars.

The densely-packed phalanx gave the Greeks a great advantage in battle.

A Greek archer — in this case, the hero Odysseus.

## Lightly Armed Troops

Most armies had javelin throwers, archers, sling-throwers and other lightly armed troops — mostly poor peasants and shopkeepers who couldn't afford hoplite arms. They could be valuable. In one battle the Athenians were beaten by javelin throwers. In the 5th century B.C., battles between Athens and Sparta and their allies used battalions of several hundred archers, slingers, and javelin throwers.

Sparta used its *helots* as bodyguards for the Spartan soldiers. At the battle of Plataea in 479 B.C., seven *helots* fought around each Spartan. This made Spartan armies almost invincible.

21

# WAR AT SEA

At the time of Homer's story *The Iliad*, ships were used to transport the soldiers to Troy. Though the oarsmen were soldiers, early "warships" were not for fighting in or for fighting other ships.

**navy:** We call a collection of ships belonging to a country and the people working for them a "navy." "Navy," "naval," and "nautical" come from the Latin *navis*, which comes from the Greek *navs* or *naos*, meaning a "ship."

### A Changing Role

After about 700 B.C., ships sometimes left harbor to stop enemy ships from reaching land. There were fights at sea between ships, and ships started to carry foot soldiers for attacking or defense. The 50-oar boats of earlier times were replaced by boats with two or three banks of oars. The *trireme*, with three banks of up to 50 oars, became the favorite Greek warship. It was quick and maneuverable, and oarsmen could fight if necessary, but the boat also carried 60 professional soldiers.

A 6th-century B.C. vase fragment of a fast warship under sail, flanked by two more.

Pointed boar's-head ram, often made of bronze

Look out and stroke

Oarsmen, low to waterline

Mast and sail

Helmsman in high swan's-neck stern

Steering oars

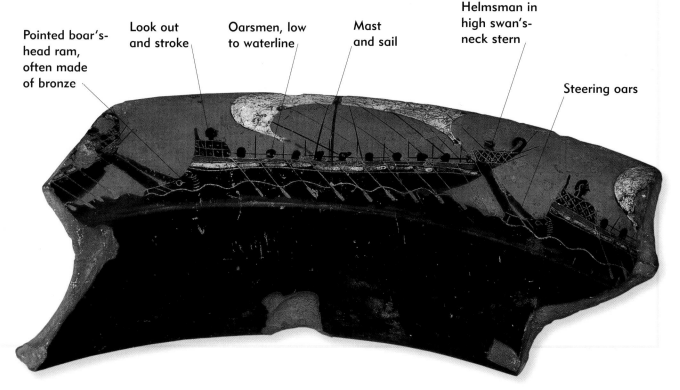

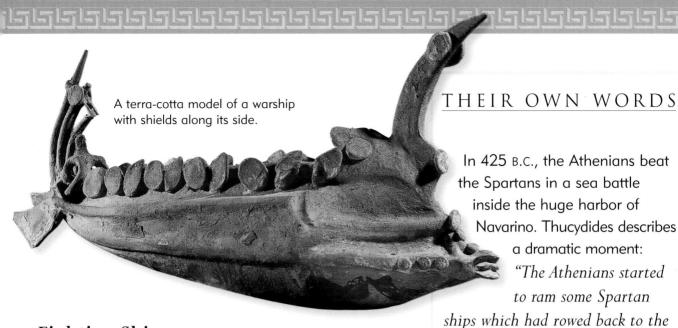

A terra-cotta model of a warship with shields along its side.

## THEIR OWN WORDS

In 425 B.C., the Athenians beat the Spartans in a sea battle inside the huge harbor of Navarino. Thucydides describes a dramatic moment:

*"The Athenians started to ram some Spartan ships which had rowed back to the shore, and some others too that were still getting their crews aboard. And they started to tow away some unmanned ships… Seeing what was happening, some of the Spartans rushed into the sea in their armor, and seized hold of the ships, trying to drag them back again."*

## Fighting Ships

By the mid-6th century B.C., sea power was a major part of warfare. Ships of war were slender and shallow-drafted, designed for speed. They improved a crucial new weapon, a metal-tipped wooden ramming spike, jutting forward from the ship just below the waterline. Real Greek sea battles began when boats started to use this fearsome weapon, giving up attacking on board in favor of ramming.

To avoid getting stuck, a ship rammed either the narrow stern or prow of the enemy's boat side-on, driving straight through and out the other side, shearing off a piece of ship.

# PERSIAN INVADERS

From the 7th century B.C., a great Persian Empire grew up to the east of the Greeks. After about 550 B.C., the Greek cities along the coast of Asia came under Persian rule. But the Persians wanted more territory and power over trade.

### Advancing into Greece

Then in 491 B.C., the Persian emperor Darius invaded Greece with about 100,000 troops and 300 to 600 ships. He conquered Thrace and Macedonia, and then in 490 B.C., his army landed in Attica. Athens sent for help to Sparta, but the Spartans didn't arrive on time. Although the Athenians were outnumbered, they defeated the Persians at Marathon. There were 192 Athenians killed, to 6,400 Persians.

A Persian archer, part of the Royal Guard.

The Athenian Treasury at Delphi contained their spoils from the Battle of Marathon.

**barbarian:** The Greeks called anyone who didn't speak Greek *barbarikos*, because they heard a meaningless noise — a bar, bar, bar, — when foreigners spoke. That became our word "barbarian," a wild person.

## Thermopylae

The second invasion was in 480 B.C., under Darius' son Xerxes. At Thermopylae, a local farmer showed the Persians a track leading from the sea up behind the mountains. When Leonidas, the Spartan king who led the Greeks, heard about this treachery, he sent all the other Greeks home and with 300 Spartans fought to the last man without any hope of winning. Xerxes marched on into Attica. The Athenians retreated to the island of Salamis, while the Persians burned down Athens.

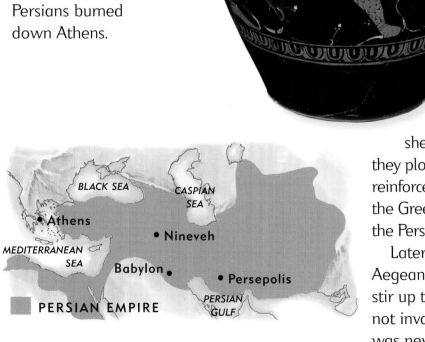

A Greek hoplite (right) fights a Persian soldier (left).

## The Battle of Salamis

But the same year at Salamis, the Persian fleet was lured toward a narrow bay. The Greek ships drove out into them, splintering their sides or sheering off ranks of Persian oars. Then they plowed into the next wave of reinforcements. The Persians lost 200 ships, the Greeks only 40. A year later, at Plataea, the Persians were beaten on land as well.

Later, Persians fought Greeks in the Aegean and gave money to Sparta to stir up trouble for Athens, but they did not invade the mainland again. Greece was never to be part of the great Persian Empire.

BLACK SEA
CASPIAN SEA
Athens
Nineveh
MEDITERRANEAN SEA
Babylon
Persepolis
PERSIAN GULF
PERSIAN EMPIRE

Map showing the Persian Empire at its greatest extent.

# WAR INSIDE GREECE

After the Persian invasions, Athens formed an alliance of states — "The Federation of Delos" — for defense if the Persians came again. But it was in effect an empire, with Athens as its leader, collecting tribute money.

## Resentment of Athens

Many cities, especially Sparta, resented Athens' growing power. Sparta formed its own league, so that Greece was split into two camps. In 431 B.C., nearly 50 years after leading the Greeks against Persia, Sparta began a war with Athens and her allies that lasted 27 years.

A bust of the Athenian leader Pericles.

Many of the buildings of the Athenian Acropolis were built with tribute money.

Athens had a great fleet, Sparta a very powerful army. They avoided each other. The Athenian leader Pericles let the Spartans take over Attica. Farmland wa abandoned to the Spartans, while the Athenians staye inside Athens. To maintain supplies, they built defenses known as the "Long Walls," between Athens and Piraeus. Plague came to the city and a quarter of the population died, including Pericles and two of his sons.

## War Becomes Brutal

Under the next Athenian leader, Cleon, the war became brutal. When Melos rebelled against Athens, the Athenians killed the men and made slaves of the women and children. When the Spartans captured Plataea in 427 B.C., they slaughtered anyone who could not prove they had been on Sparta's side.

A soldier straps on his sword. His shield and helmet lie ready.

## Fighting at Sea

For most of the war, Athenian ships kept the grain routes from the Black Sea safe. But more and more of Athens' allies broke away. In the end, Athens was fighting to protect its grain route.

In the last years of the war, Sparta was helped by Persian money. They built their own fleet and in 405 B.C. won a victory at sea. After that, Athens could not protect its grain ships. So in the winter of 404 B.C., its citizens starving, Athens was forced to surrender.

# PHILIP AND ALEXANDER

**I**n the 4th century B.C., Greece slowly weakened itself with more wars. Something needed to be done. Two great Greek leaders, father and son, worked to make Greece strong again.

## Philip II

Between 357 and 336 B.C., Philip II, King of Macedon, Thebes and Athens, gradually overpowered all of Greece with his huge armies. Philip had full-time soldiers. He thought up new tactics and tougher training. Philip planned to invade Persia, to punish it, he said, for Darius' invasion 150 years before. He probably had his eye on the gold and riches of Asia too. But after announcing his plan, he was murdered.

A gold medalion showing Philip II of Macedonia, conqueror of Greece.

## Alexander the Great

Philip II's son, Alexander, inherited a united Greece from his father. He took over the army and crossed into Asia. He craved fame but also had enormous debts to pay off. He needed the wealth of Asia and to control its trading links. Marching south, Alexander won many battles.

In a mosaic from Pompeii, Italy, Alexander fights the Persians at the Battle of Issus, 333 B.C.

Thousands of paid soldiers created widespread destruction, sometimes of whole cities. Bigger warships and new inventions — like siege catapults and movable towers — were used. Alexander defeated Darius, the Persian emperor, and took his gold. He marched on to modern Afghanistan, into India, and back along the Persian Gulf. He covered amazing distances with a huge army and cavalry. Alexander died in Babylon in 323 B.C., aged 32, but he left an extraordinary legacy behind.

**catapult:** Our word is from the Greek word *katapeltis*, made by combining *kata*, "against," and *peltis* a "shield." Perhaps the Greek catapult was designed especially to damage shields.

Map showing the extent of Alexander's empire and the route of his armies.

ALEXANDER'S EMPIRE
ROUTE OF HIS ARMY

### A New Greek World

Everywhere he went, Alexander founded cities, laying them out in a Greek grid plan, with Greek buildings like theaters and gymnasiums. To this new world, the Greeks took all their learning, arts, and technology. The silk route from China led directly into the Greek-Indian kingdom of Bactria. Scents and spices, gold and luxury goods poured in. From trade and warfare, a new Greek civilization, known as the Hellenistic, was born — an extraordinary mixture of European, African, and Asiatic cultures.

Alexander sculpted to resemble a god. He encouraged people to worship and adore him like a god.

29

# GLOSSARY

**Afghanistan:** the country lying between modern Iran and Pakistan.

**alabaster:** an attractive hard white rock that can be carved into objects, such as lamps or boxes.

**Aristotle (384–322 B.C.):** a famous philosopher and writer. He wrote about many things, including politics, science, and how people behave. He thought men naturally fought, plundered, and "hunted" each other.

**Babylon:** Major city and center of power in the ancient world, located on the River Euphrates in what is now Iraq.

**Bactria:** an ancient kingdom in the north of modern Afghanistan.

**bronze:** a metal alloy (blend) of mainly copper with some tin to strengthen it.

**city-state:** a small state that included a city at its center and the surrounding countryside and villages. From about 800 to 400 B.C., Greece was divided into a series of city-states, each with their own laws, systems of government, and coinage.

**Cleon (died 422 B.C.):** ruler of Athens after Pericles. The son of a wealthy tanner, his policies led to Athens' defeat by Sparta.

**colony:** a settlement of people who have left their own homes to live somewhere else. After about 800 B.C., Greek cities sent out many colonists.

**Darius (reigned 522-486 B.C.):** the emperor of Persia (Achaemenid dynasty) who invaded Greece in 491.

**gymnasium:** a sports center with all kinds of equipment and facilities for track and field events. Wherever they went, the Greeks built gymnasiums.

**helot:** a slave from Messenia, who served the Spartans, giving them farm produce, manual labor, and military service.

**Herodotus (c. 480-425 B.C.):** sometimes called the first historian, Herodotus wrote about the wars between the Greeks and Persians. He traveled all over the Greek world, collecting information about different peoples and customs.

# TIME LINE

| | |
|---|---|
| c. 8000 B.C. | Early trade across Aegean, for example in flint. |
| c. 3000 | Greek bronze being made. |
| c. 1500 | Mycenaeans trading. |
| c. 1200 | Mycenaean palaces burned. |
| c. 1100 | Greeks begin to migrate to coast of Asia (modern Turkey) — "Ionian" Greece. |
| c. 1050 | Iron being used for weapons and tools. |
| c. 1000-750 | Phoenicians prosperous, traveling and trading. |
| c. 900-750 | Trade in "geometric" vases. |

| | |
|---|---|
| c. 800 | Greeks trading from Al Mina, Syria, North Africa, and Egypt. |
| c. 800-500 | Greeks settling all around Mediterranean and Black Sea. |
| 776 | Traditional date for first all-Greece Olympic Games. |
| c. 750-700 | Homer composes his poems. |
| c. 750 | Greeks borrow and adapt Phoenician alphabet. |
| 750 on | Heavy hoplite armor being used. |

| | |
|---|---|
| 735 | First Sicilian colony, Naxos. |
| 733 | Corkyra and Syracuse founded by Corinth. |
| 730-710 | Spartans conquer and enslave Messenians. |
| c. 700 | Athens combines with towns of Attica to make one city-state. |
| c. 700 | Poet Hesiod composing. |
| 630 | Cyrene founded in Africa. |
| c. 600 | Founding of Massalia. |
| c. 600 | First battles at sea. |

**Homer (c. 8th century B.C.):** the blind poet who composed two great story-poems, *The Iliad* and *The Odyssey*, about the Greeks' war with the Trojans, and their return home.

**hoplite:** a heavily armed foot soldier, who fought with other hoplites in a tight phalanx.

**Lydia:** a large civilized country lying behind the coastal Greek settlements in Ionia (part of modern Turkey). Its king was Croesus.

**Magna Graecia:** "Great Greece" was the name given to the part of Sicily and southern Italy colonized by Greeks.

**ore:** the raw material for a metal. For instance, iron ore is mined and iron extracted from it.

**Peloponnese:** the large area of land in the south of Greece, below the Gulf of Corinth.

**Pericles (c. 495–429 B.C.):** leader of Athens from about 454 to 429. He was responsible for the rebuilding of Athens after the Persian invasion.

**Persian Empire:** the empire with its center in modern Iran that invaded Greece in the 5th century B.C. Also known as the Achaemenid Empire, after its ruling family.

**phalanx:** a square fight formation made up of rows of hoplite soldiers.

**Phoenicians:** people from the eastern Mediterranean (modern Lebanon and part of Syria) who were successful traders and travelers from about 1050 B.C. onward.

**Sparta:** the chief city-state of the Peloponnese, in southern Greece, and often Athens' rival and enemy. Sparta was famed for its obsession with war and the tough way it brought up children.

**Thucydides (c. 455–400 B.C.):** a general in the Athenian army, who wrote a famous history of the war between Athens and Sparta and their allies. The war was later called the Peloponnesian War.

**Trireme:** ship with three rows of oarsmen. Each row sat on benches at different levels, using oars of different lengths. A *trireme* might have 150 oarsmen.

**Xerxes (reigned 486–465 B.C.):** a Persian king, the son of Darius. Xerxes invaded Greece in 480.

| | |
|---|---|
| after 600 | Coins begin to circulate. |
| 545 | Persia conquers Ionians. |
| 493 | Rich strike of silver at Laurium, in Attica, pays for warships to be built. |
| 491 | First Persian invasion, under Darius — Greek victory at Marathon. |
| 480 | Second Persian invasion, under Xerxes — Greeks beaten at Thermopylae. Athens burned by Persians; Greeks win at Salamis. |
| 479 | Greeks win at Platea; Persians go home. |
| 461 | Pericles leader in Athens. |
| 449 | Peace of Callias — wars with Persia officially ended. |
| c.445-426 | Herodotus writing. |
| 431-404 | War between Athens and Sparta (Peloponnesian War). |
| 431 | Thucydides starts writing. |
| 429 | Pericles dies of plague. |
| 425 | Athenians beat Spartans at Pylos — Spartan offer of peace refused by Cleon. |
| 425 | Aristophanes' first anti-war play produced. |
| 404 | Athens surrenders to Sparta. |
| 357-336 | Philip II of Macedon extends power over all mainland Greece. |
| 336 | Death of Philip. |
| 334 | Alexander crosses into Asia. |
| 333-324 | Alexander's victorious campaigns in Egypt, Persia, India. |
| 323 | Death of Alexander. |

# INDEX